Fine Feathered Friends

classify science terms
✓ W9-CPF-550

Name _____

Use the words from the Word Box to build a puzzle.

Hint: Build off **woodpecker** first.

| W | O | O | D | P | E | C | K | E | R |

Word Box

jay	eagle	pigeon	woodpecker
owl	crow	parrot	cardinal
robin	falcon		

Picture This

Name _____

Color the picture the bold-faced word tells about.

	I will **coast** to the bottom of the hill.	
	The teacher said to **pass** the room quietly.	
	Barb lost the dollar **bill** she needed for lunch.	
	The **glass** was shattered.	
	Don is my **hero**.	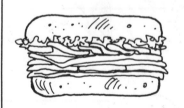
	Can you **field** a ball as good as Carlos?	

     IF5022 Vocabulary Enrichment

Mitten Match

Name _____

If the words on the pairs of mittens mean nearly the same thing, color the mittens. If they do not, put an **X** on the mittens.

Do You Know the Code?

Name _____

Use the code to write an antonym for each word.

t	r	s
c	h	a
n	e	i

Example: thick → ⌟ ☐ ⌌ ⌐ = thin

1. there → ☐ ⌐ ⌎ ⌐   = _____

2. poor → ⌎ ⌌ ⌐ ☐   = _____

3. messy → ⌐ ⌐ ☐ ⌟   = _____

4. work → ⌎ ⌐ ⌞ ☐   = _____

5. unpleasant → ⌐ ⌌ ☐ ⌐   = _____

6. basement → ☐ ⌟ ⌟ ⌌ ⌐   = _____

7. throw → ⌐ ☐ ⌟ ⌟ ☐   = _____

IF5022 Vocabulary Enrichment

Palindromes — Wow!

Name _____

A palindrome is a word that reads the same forward and backward. Use the code to write a palindrome for each word or phrase.

Example: short for sister = $\dfrac{S}{9}$ $\dfrac{I}{4}$ $\dfrac{S}{9}$

Code	1	2	3	4	5	6	7	8	9	10	11
	a	d	e	i	m	n	o	p	s	t	u

1. mother = $\dfrac{}{5}$ $\dfrac{}{7}$ $\dfrac{}{5}$

2. father = $\dfrac{}{2}$ $\dfrac{}{1}$ $\dfrac{}{2}$

3. energy = $\dfrac{}{8}$ $\dfrac{}{3}$ $\dfrac{}{8}$

4. burst = $\dfrac{}{8}$ $\dfrac{}{7}$ $\dfrac{}{8}$

5. young dog = $\dfrac{}{8}$ $\dfrac{}{11}$ $\dfrac{}{8}$

6. past tense of do = $\dfrac{}{2}$ $\dfrac{}{4}$ $\dfrac{}{2}$

7. midday = $\dfrac{}{6}$ $\dfrac{}{7}$ $\dfrac{}{7}$ $\dfrac{}{6}$

8. horn blast = $\dfrac{}{10}$ $\dfrac{}{7}$ $\dfrac{}{7}$ $\dfrac{}{10}$

At the Beach

Name _____

If the two words on a shell make a compound word, write them together on a line. Put an **X** on the shell if they do not make a compound word.

Write a compound word from the list that is a synonym for beach.

_____

In a Nutshell

Name _____

Use the words from the Word Bank to build a puzzle.

Hint: Build off **chestnut** first.

Word Bank

acorn	pecan	almond	cashew
peanut	walnut	filbert	chestnut

Unscramble the letters to find another name for a filbert. Write it on the line.

_____

See You Later, Alligator

Name _____

If the pair of words on the alligator rhyme, color the alligator. If the words do not rhyme, put an **X** on the alligator.

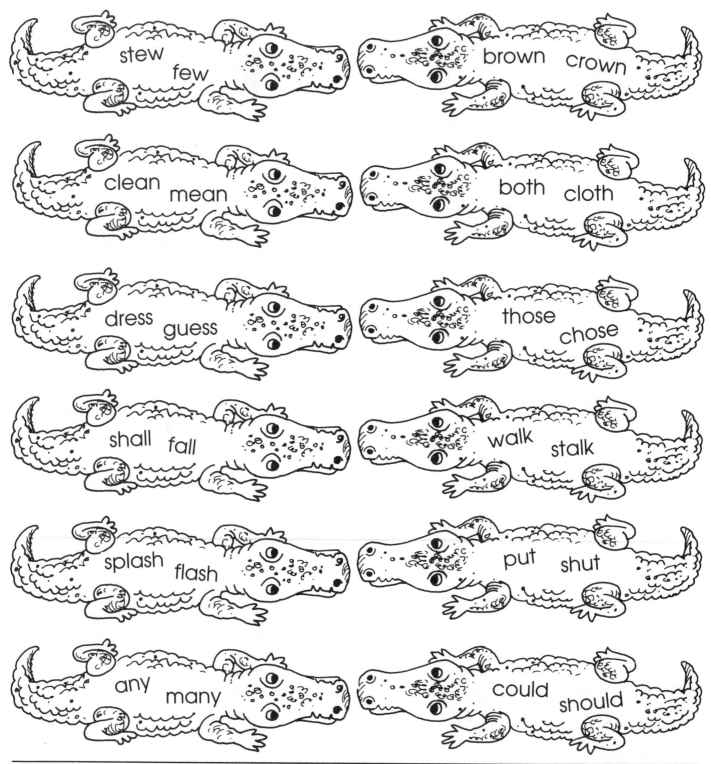

stew few

brown crown

clean mean

both cloth

dress guess

those chose

shall fall

walk stalk

splash flash

put shut

any many

could should

A Day with Clay

Name _____

Choose the word that means nearly the same as the underlined word to complete each sentence. Write it in the blank.

I hope we <u>start</u> our art project today.

I want to _____ work now.
(begin, stop)

If I <u>finish</u> my clay bowl quickly, I'll have

time to _____ a vase, too.
(company, complete)

I'll <u>send</u> the bowl to Grandma

and _____ the vase to Aunt Sue.
(mail, take)

Grandma could <u>place</u> the bowl on her

table or _____ it on a shelf.
(sit, set)

Which Will You Pick?

Name _____

Rewrite each sentence, replacing the bold-faced word with another word that has the same meaning.

Word	Meanings	
peep	1. sound	2. look
pick	1. choose	2. gather
soft	1. low	2. not hard

1. My pillow is **soft.**

   _____

2. Please **pick** me for the team.

   _____

3. Can you **peep** over the fence?

   _____

4. Hear the **soft** call of the dove.

   _____

5. Sasha will **pick** flowers.

   _____

6. Did you hear the **peep** of the chick?

   _____

   _____

Unsolved Mystery

Name _____

If the pair of words on the magnifying glass are antonyms, write the letter from the handle above the matching numeral in the coded message. Put an **X** on the word pairs that are not antonyms.

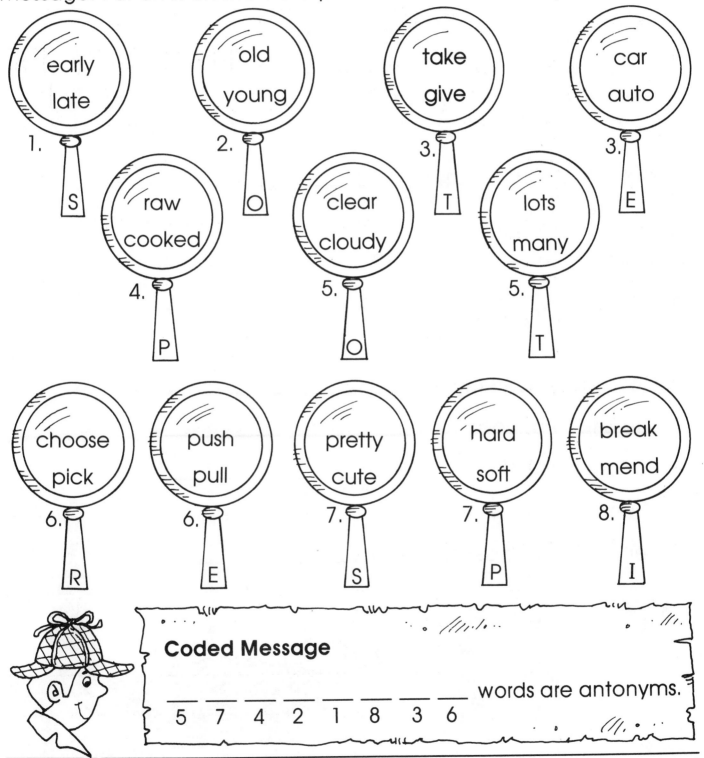

Coded Message

___ ___ ___ ___ ___ ___ ___ ___ words are antonyms.
5   7   4   2   1   8   3   6

Analyze These Analogies

Name _____

Write the correct word from the Word Box to complete each analogy.

Word Box				
eat	oink	brook	scales	color
sail	after	swamp	person	lemon

1. Gas is to car as food is to _____ .

2. Milk is to drink as bread is to _____ .

3. Bee is to hive as alligator is to _____ .

4. Hard is to soft as before is to _____ .

5. Bear is to fur as fish is to _____ .

6. Cow is to moo as pig is to _____ .

7. Kite is to fly as boat is to _____ .

8. Road is to street as creek is to _____ .

9. Green is to lime as yellow is to _____ .

10. Pencil is to write as crayon is to _____ .

Home Sweet Home

Name _____

Write the name of each animal's home below its picture. Then complete each sentence with the correct word.

Word Box					
hive	hutch	kennel	nest	stable	sty

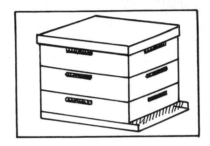

_____ _____ _____

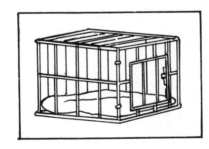

_____ _____ _____

1. Bees live in a _____ .

2. Our dog is in its _____ .

3. The robin is in the _____ .

4. My horse is in its _____ .

5. Two pigs are in the _____ .

6. Can you see the rabbit's _____ ?

Draw each animal in its home in the pictures above.

How Do You Feel About This?

Name _____

In each oval, write a word from the Word Box that tells about the main idea.

Word Box

sad	upset	grumpy	unhappy
glad	happy	loving	worried
caring	angry	joyful	cheerful

When I feel good about myself, I am . . .

When I don't feel good about myself, I am . . .

IF5022 Vocabulary Enrichment

Try Hard on This

Name _____

Write the number of the correct definition for the bold-faced word in each sentence.

> **bite** (bīt) 1. cut with teeth
> 2. a piece bitten off 3. a sore from a bite

____ 1. Don't scratch that mosquito **bite**.

____ 2. Would you like a **bite** of my brownie?

____ 3. It's hard to **bite** into this apple because of my loose tooth.

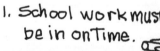
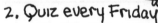

> **hard** (härd) 1. not soft 2. strict
> 3. not easily done

____ 1. Weeding the garden is **hard** work.

____ 2. The ground is **hard**.

____ 3. Mrs. Applegate certainly is a **hard** teacher.

You Don't Say!

Name _____

Rewrite the sentences using **announced**, **answered**, **asked**, **begged** or **yelled** instead of **said**.

	"May I please speak to Bob?" **said** Joel. _____ _____ _____
	"I'm sorry, but Bob is at the ball game," **said** his sister. _____ _____ _____
	"Please, Coach, give me a chance to bat," **said** Bob. _____ _____ _____
	"The pinch-hitter is Bob Garcia," **said** the announcer. _____ _____ _____
	"Get a hit!" **said** the fans. _____ _____

Yummy for the Tummy

Name _____

Write the words from the Word Box under the correct category name. Then circle the words in the wordsearch. Look ↑ ↓ → ← ↘ ↙ .

Word Box			
apple	carrot	orange	peas
banana	cherry	peach	potato
beans	corn	pear	squash

Fruits   **Vegetables**

_____ _____   _____ _____

_____ _____   _____ _____

_____ _____   _____ _____

P E G N A R O L O
S A P P L E W R S
T N R O C P N Q S
O A R N T E U O H
R N A S N A E B C
R A E M S S T L A
A B P H K E N O E
C H E R R Y A T P

Eating Out

Name _____

Circle the correct word and write it in the blank.

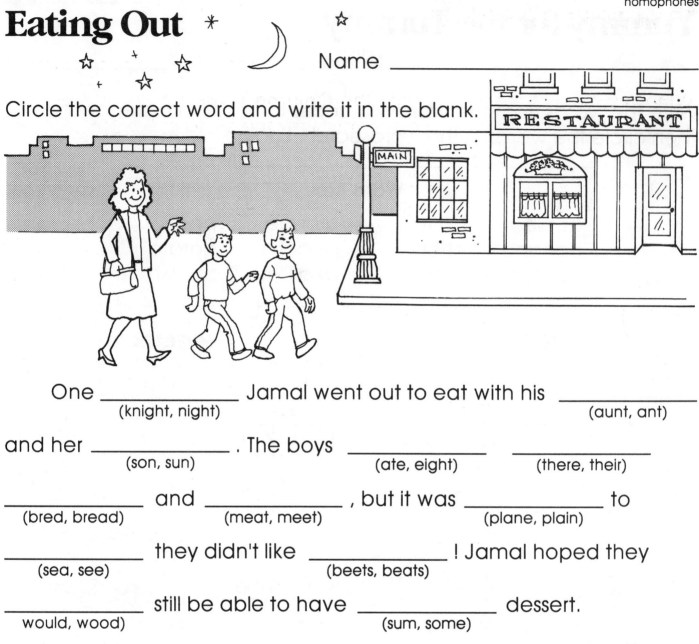

One _____ Jamal went out to eat with his _____
    (knight, night)   (aunt, ant)

and her _____ . The boys _____ _____
    (son, sun)   (ate, eight)   (there, their)

_____ and _____ , but it was _____ to
(bred, bread)   (meat, meet)   (plane, plain)

_____ they didn't like _____ ! Jamal hoped they
(sea, see)   (beets, beats)

_____ still be able to have _____ dessert.
would, wood)   (sum, some)

Unscramble the letters to find out what Jamal wanted for dessert.
Write it on the line.

_____

       18   IF5022 Vocabulary Enrichment

Synonym Switch

Name _____

Write a synonym for the word in the **Column 1**. Then change one letter in that word to make a synonym for the word in **Column 2**.

Example:

father
| d | a | d |

mean
| b | a | d |

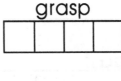

Column 1   ## Column 2

1. cool
| | | | |

grasp
| | | | |

2. carnival
| | | | |

den
| | | | |

3. remain
| | | | |

swing
| | | | |

4. tale
| | | | |

shop
| | | | |

5. look
| | | | |

extra
| | | | |

6. powerful
| | | | | | |

cord
| | | | |

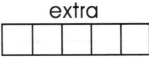

Word Problems

Name _____

Use words from the Word Box to complete these word equations. Add two words that go with the first two words. Then write the category name as the sum.

Word Box

behind	locations	postcard	aunt
sweater	messages	relatives	uncle
clothes	middle	slacks	card

Example: north   +   **east** _____

south   +   **west** _____   =   **directions** _____

1. grandmother + _____

   cousin   + _____   =   _____

2. center   + _____

   ahead   + _____   =   _____

3. note   + _____

   letter   + _____   =   _____

4. skirt   + _____

   dress   + _____   =   _____

IF5022 Vocabulary Enrichment

What Does It Mean?

Name _____

Read the meanings given for each word. Write the number of the correct meaning of each bold-faced word in the circle.

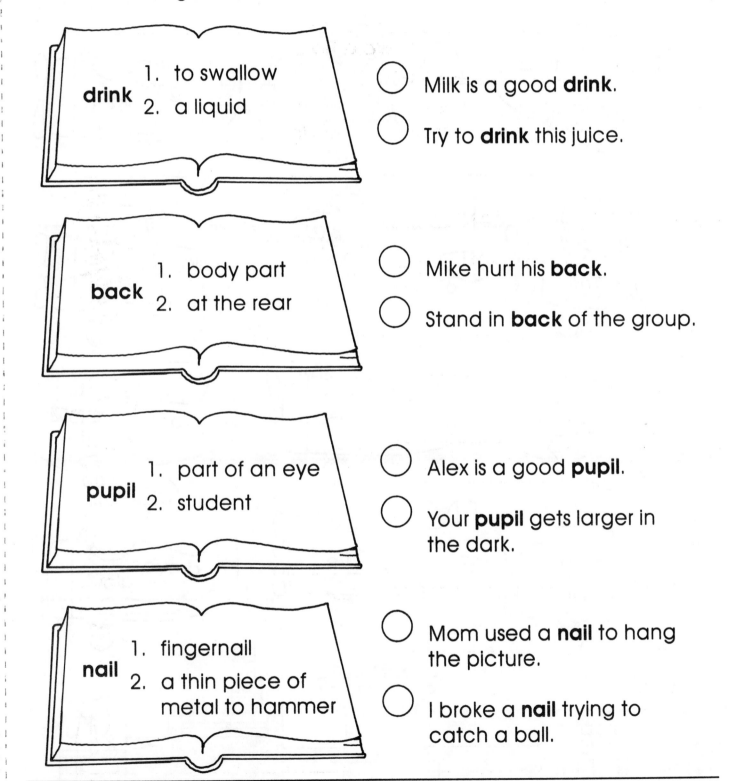

drink
1. to swallow
2. a liquid

◯ Milk is a good **drink**.

◯ Try to **drink** this juice.

back
1. body part
2. at the rear

◯ Mike hurt his **back**.

◯ Stand in **back** of the group.

pupil
1. part of an eye
2. student

◯ Alex is a good **pupil**.

◯ Your **pupil** gets larger in the dark.

nail
1. fingernail
2. a thin piece of metal to hammer

◯ Mom used a **nail** to hang the picture.

◯ I broke a **nail** trying to catch a ball.

High in the Sky

Name _____

If the pair of words on the plane rhyme, color the plane. If they do not, put an **X** on it.

Right or Wrong?

Name _____

Write the antonym from the Word Box for each word below. Then circle the words from the Word Box in the wordsearch. Words may go ↑ ↓ → ← ↘ .

Word Box				
above	find	light	lower	weak
fancy	huge	love	shut	wrong

1. dark _____

2. right _____

3. tiny _____

4. raise _____

5. hate _____

6. below _____

7. strong _____

8. plain _____

9. lose _____

10. open _____

```
M T U H S W Y
L T L O V E C
O D N I F A N
W R O N G K A
E S E G U H F
R A B O V E T
```

Let's See That Smile

Name _____

Color each tube of toothpaste that names something in the picture.

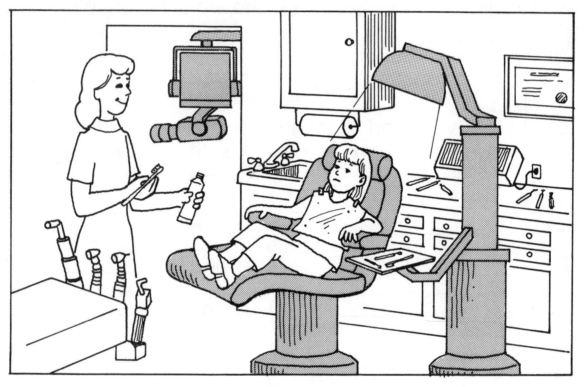

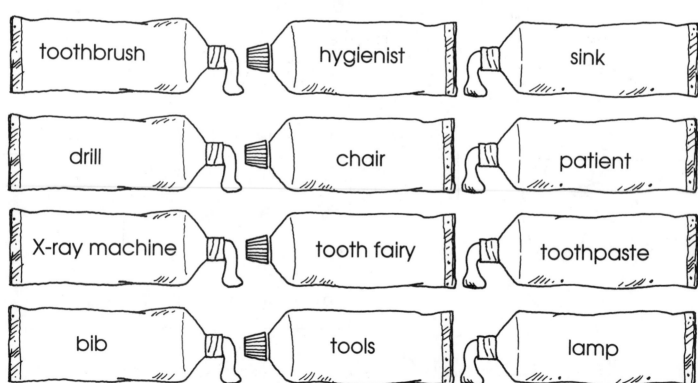

toothbrush | hygienist | sink

drill | chair | patient

X-ray machine | tooth fairy | toothpaste

bib | tools | lamp

Here's the Scoop!

Name _____

On each blank, write a word from the Word Box that comes between the other two words in alphabetical order.

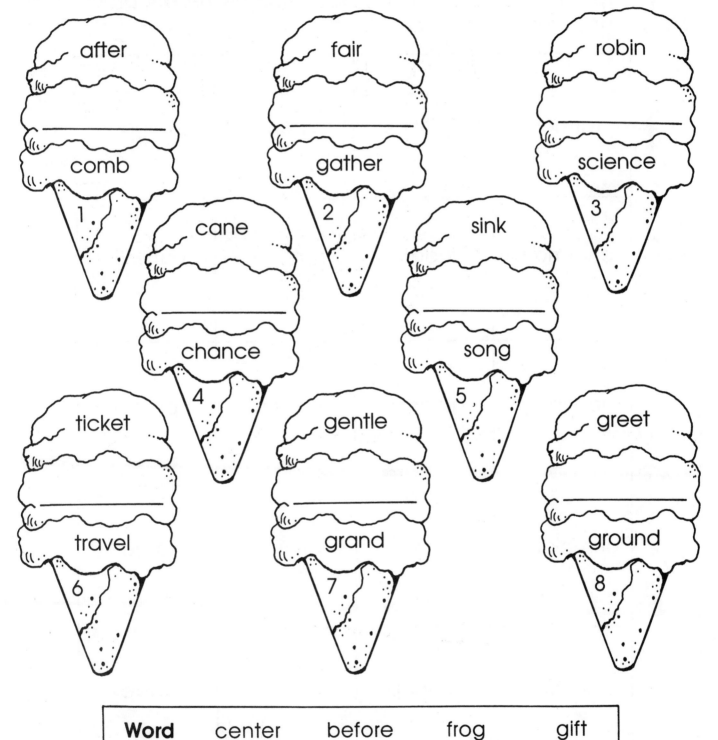

after
_____
comb
1

fair
_____
gather
2

robin
_____
science
3

cane
_____
chance
4

sink
_____
song
5

ticket
_____
travel
6

gentle
_____
grand
7

greet
_____
ground
8

Word	center	before	frog	gift
Box	salad	touch	grind	slide

Follow Me

Name _____

Circle the words that name types of work. Underline the words that are synonyms for big. Color the boxes that name insects. Draw a heart around words that name sweets.

farmer	fly	cupcake	huge
enormous	fudge	butcher	butterfly
ladybug	gigantic	cookie	painter
bumblebee	artist	cricket	large
jumbo	lollipop	dancer	cake

Simple Similes

Name _____

Write a word from the Word Box to complete each simile.

Word Box			
dry	sweet	strong	stubborn
light	lovely	quiet	sparkled
quick	cuddly		

1. The children were as _____ as

2. Mr. Jones is as _____ as a

3. My throat is as _____ as a

4. Susan is as _____ as a

5. John Henry was as _____ as an

6. My teddy bear is as _____ as a

7. I finished my work as _____ as a

8. The lake _____ like 💎💎 in the sun.

9. This paper is as _____ as a

10. Kevin was as _____ as

Use Your Head on This One!

Name _____

Choose words from the Word Box to match each clue and complete the puzzle.

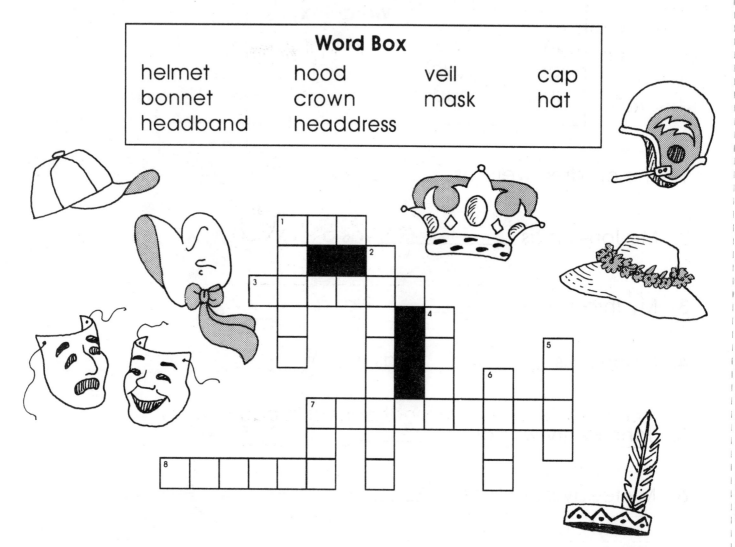

Word Box

helmet	hood	veil	cap
bonnet	crown	mask	hat
headband	headdress		

Across

1. head covering with bill
3. worn by a baby
7. worn by Native American chiefs
8. worn by a football player

Down

1. worn by a king or queen
2. worn to hold back hair
4. head covering that is part of a coat
5. worn to cover the face
6. worn by a bride
7. head covering with a brim

Pyramid of Health

Name _____

People in the 1990's are trying to eat healthier meals. This pyramid shows a new way to make food choices every day. You should eat more of the foods at the bottom of the pyramid and less at the top.

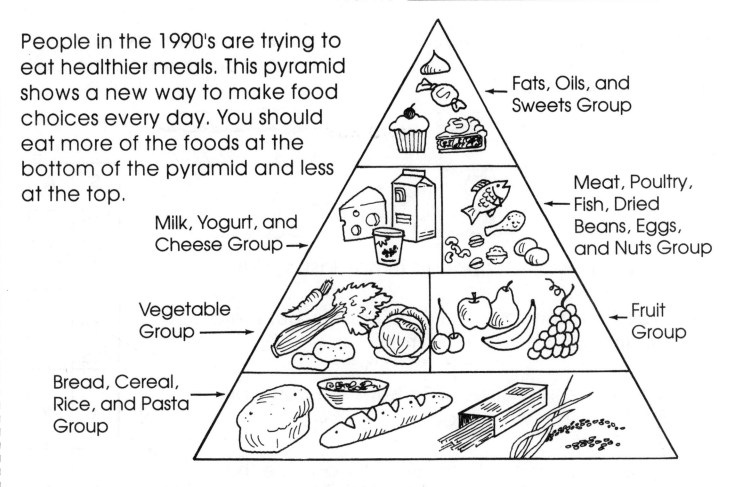

Fats, Oils, and Sweets Group

Meat, Poultry, Fish, Dried Beans, Eggs, and Nuts Group

Milk, Yogurt, and Cheese Group →

Fruit Group

Vegetable Group →

Bread, Cereal, Rice, and Pasta Group →

Cross out the word that does not belong in each group.

1.	cake	butter	fudge	rice
2.	walnuts	cream	chicken	beef
3.	eggs	cottage cheese	milk	yogurt
4.	plums	grapes	cabbage	bananas
5.	lettuce	carrots	celery	strawberries
6.	crackers	cookies	cornbread	bagel

This Isn't Puzzling to Me!

Name _____

Read each sentence. If the pair of bold-faced words are **synonyms**, circle the letter in the **S** column. If the words are **antonyms**, circle the letter in the **A** column.

	S	A
1.	e	t
2.	s	c
3.	i	w
4.	e	r
5.	m	p

1. It **looks** like rain. It **appears** it may last all day.

2. We had **many** things to do outdoors, but there are **few** we can do in the rain.

3. **Maybe** we'll stay inside. **Perhaps** we can work on the puzzle we started.

4. If we finish the **whole** puzzle, we can glue the **entire** thing and frame it.

5. Then we'll have a picture to **remember** the good time we had making it. I don't want to **forget** that.

Write the circled letters above the matching numerals to spell the answer to the following question.

What is the one thing you never want
to lose when doing a puzzle?   a __ __ __ __ __
                                    5 3 1 2 4

Piece Is to Puzzle

Name _____

Write a word in each puzzle to complete each analogy.

1. In is to out as stop is to . . .

2. She is to her as he is to . . .

3. House is to build as well is to . . .

4. Dog is to bark as lion is to . . .

5. Ceiling is to room as lid is to . . .

6. Much is to little as early is to . . .

The Solar System

Name _____

Cut out and paste each picture by the correct sentence. Then write the name of each picture.

1. The bright heavenly bodies seen in the sky at night. _____

2. The center of our solar system. _____

3. It rotates on its axis once every 24 hours. _____

4. It revolves around the Earth once about every 28 days. _____

5. Our sun and its planets are all part of the Milky Way. _____

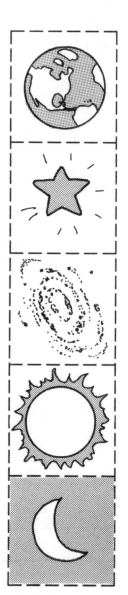

Word Bank		
Earth	galaxy	moon
sun	stars	

Checkerboard Square

Name _____

In each box, color the circle green if the pair of words makes a compound word. Color the circle red if they do not.

○	○	○	○	○
wind mill	over here	my house	pan cake	lamp light
○	○	○	○	○
some toys	lady bug	ginger bread	dew drop	bed spread
○	○	○	○	○
candle light	beauty full	play ground	wood chuck	once upon
○	○	○	○	○
shoe maker	straw berry	out doors	after this	hill top
○	○	○	○	○
two day	paper weight	sky scraper	sand paper	shoe lace

This Drives Me Batty!

Name _____

If the pair of words on the bat rhyme, color the bat. If they do not, put an **X** on it.

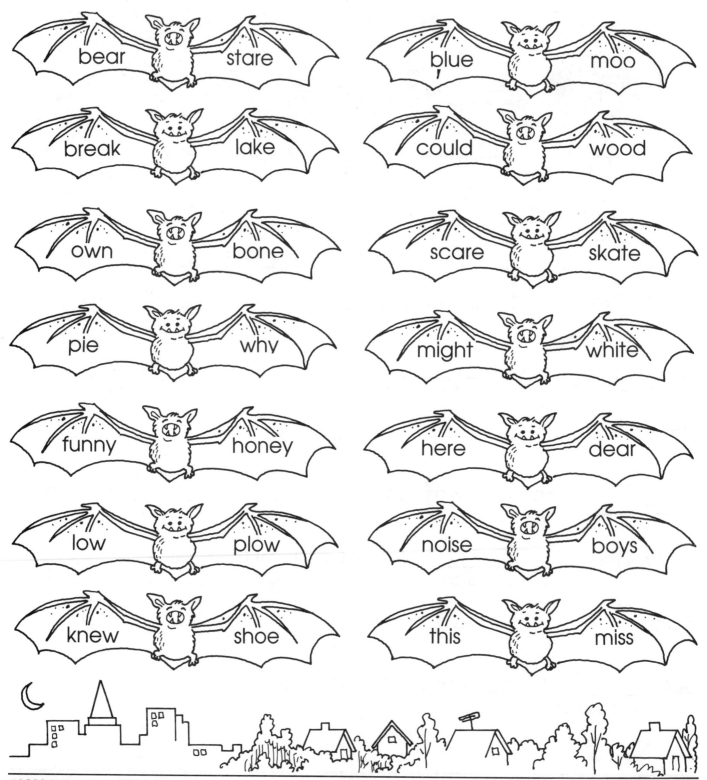

bear · stare

blue · moo

break · lake

could · wood

own · bone

scare · skate

pie · why

might · white

funny · honey

here · dear

low · plow

noise · boys

knew · shoe

this · miss

IF5022 Vocabulary Enrichment

Once Upon a Time

Name _____

Circle the correct word and write it in the blank.

Mr. Hill, the librarian, read _____ class a story about a
(hour, our)

_____ and a _____ godmother. We _____ a
(prince, prints)   (ferry, fairy)   (knew, new)

story about a godmother, but _____ never _____ this
(weed, we'd)   (herd, heard)

_____ before. It was such a _____ _____ that
(won, one)   (great, grate)   (tale, tail)

we weren't _____ . We asked Mr. Hill to let us _____
(bored, board)   (hear, here)

it again. He said that we had _____ good listeners, but he
(bin, been)

did _____ have time to read it again.
(not, knot)

Join the Community

Name _____

Use words from the Word Box to complete each sentence. Then write those words in the puzzle.

Word Box

council   laws   taxes
problems   rules   mayor
leaders   city   vote
services

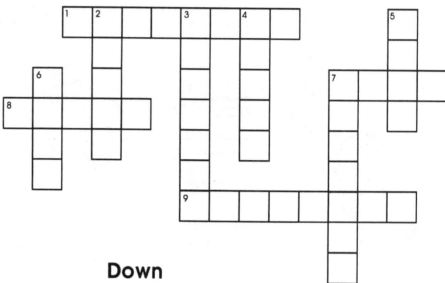

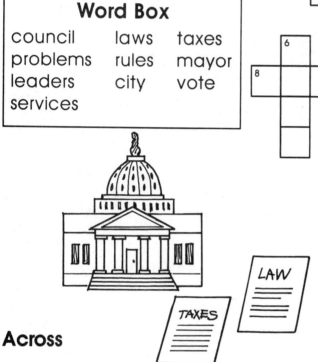

Across

1. One job of a community group is to try to solve

_____ .

7. The community's mayor may

work at a _____ hall.

8. _____ pay for

community services.

9. A community provides many

_____ .

Down

2. Communities follow strict

_____ .

3. Communities have people who

are _____ .

4. A community may elect a

_____ .

5. People _____ for leaders and laws.

6. _____ help govern communities.

7. A _____ is a group of community lawmakers.

Unlock These Words

Name _____

Write the pronunciation for each word in bold-faced type.

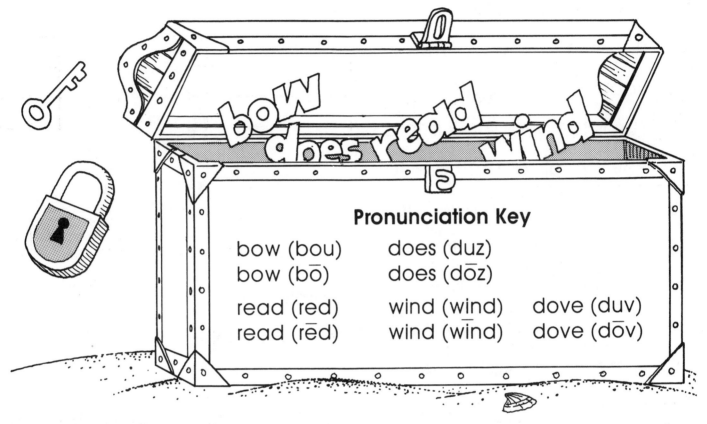

Pronunciation Key

bow (bou)   does (duz)
bow (bō)   does (dōz)

read (red)   wind (wind)   dove (duv)
read (rēd)   wind (wīnd)   dove (dōv)

1. The hunter **does** (_____) not see the two **does** (_____).

2. I'll **read** (_____) this book after I've **read** (_____) that one.

3. Jill's **bow** (_____) fell off when she took a **bow** (_____).

4. The **wind** (_____) caused the flag to **wind** (_____) around the pole.

5. The **dove** (_____) **dove** (_____) to pick up the seed.

You'll Shine on This!

Name _____

Write a word from the design to complete each analogy. Write it.
Then color that word's space yellow.

1. Puppy is to dog as kitten is to _____ .

2. Boot is to foot as glove is to _____ .

3. Sun is to hot as snow is to _____ .

4. Boy is to girl as brother is to _____ .

5. Den is to bear as hive is to _____ .

6. Breakfast is to morning as dinner is to _____ .

7. Bird is to sky as fish is to _____ .

8. Pretty is to lovely as wise is to _____ .

9. Fast is to slow as high is to _____ .

10. Plane is to pilot as car is to _____ .

Color the remaining spaces blue.

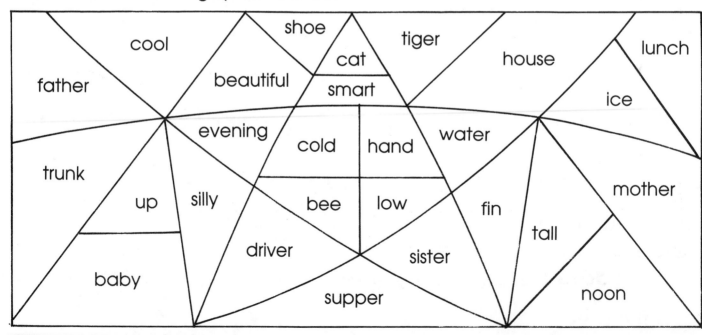

Batter Up!

Name _____

Read the meanings given for each word. On the line, write the
correct meaning of the word as it is used in each sentence.

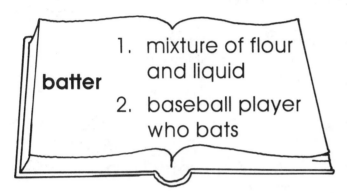

1. Dawn is the next **batter**.

_____

_____

2. Dad poured the **batter** on
the griddle.

_____

_____

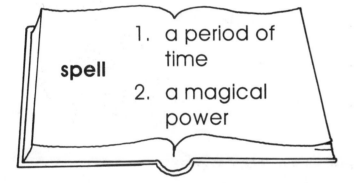

3. The long dry **spell** ended
yesterday.

_____

4. The wizard's **spell** turned the
toad into a frog.

_____

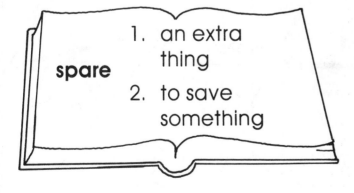

5. Please **spare** the rain forests.

_____

6. Mother keeps a **spare** tire in
the trunk.

_____

This Is Pretty Nice!

Name _____

Find a new word from the Word Box to use instead of the bold-faced word in each sentence. Write the new words in the puzzle.

Word Box			
cute	lovely	enjoyable	attractive
fine	proper	adorable	beautiful
kind	pleasing		

Across

3. Marla is a **pretty** girl.
6. That kitten is **pretty**.
7. That is not a **nice** way to behave!
8. You are so **nice** to me.
9. The new curtains are **pretty**.
10. That rose is **pretty**.

Down

1. What a **pretty** baby!
2. That painting is **nice** to look at.
4. This is a **nice** picnic.
5. Eric is a **nice** person.

IF5022 Vocabulary Enrichment

As Tough As Nails

Name _____

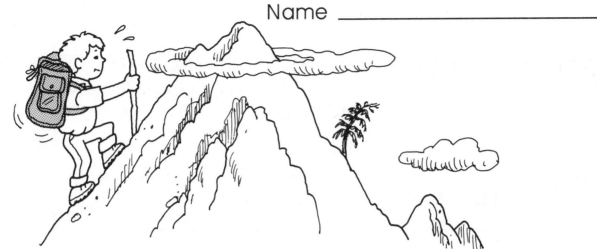

Write a word from the Word Box to complete each simile.

Word Box

big	hot	heavy	jumpy	rough
slow	tough	smart	white	smooth

1. That house is as _____ as a barn.

2. He's as _____ as a whip!

3. This room is as _____ as an oven.

4. The line moved as _____ as a snail.

5. My backpack is as _____ as a rock.

6. The boy is as _____ as a jackrabbit.

7. Alice's hair is as _____ as silk.

8. Anton is as _____ as nails.

9. My hands are as _____ as sandpaper.

10. Suddenly, John's face turned as _____ as a sheet.

Super Synonyms

Name _____

Use words from the Word Box to write synonyms for each pair of words. Then write each numbered letter in the box with the same number. You'll spell a synonym for the word above the boxes.

Word Box			
assist	right	similar	trip
rescue	weird	fearless	silly

strange — — — — —
         1 2 3 4 5

journey — — — —
         6 4 3 7

sleepy

☐ ☐ ☐ ☐ ☐
6 3 4 2 5

brave — — — — — — — —
       1 2 3 4 5 2 6 6

help — — — — — —
      3 6 6 7 6 8

steps

☐ ☐ ☐ ☐ ☐ ☐
6 8 3 7 4 6

foolish — — — — —
         1 2 3 3 4

save — — — — — —
      5 6 1 7 8 6

ring

☐ ☐ ☐ ☐ ☐ ☐
7 2 5 7 3 6

correct — — — — —
        1 2 3 4 5

alike — — — — — — — —
       6 2 7 2 8 9 1

wise

☐ ☐ ☐ ☐ ☐
6 7 9 1 5

       IF5022 Vocabulary Enrichment

Marvelous Magnets

Name _____

Some things are pulled, or **attracted**, by a magnet. Other **objects** are not. Because **magnetism** is **invisible**, you cannot tell if an object is magnetic just by looking at it. Things **containing** mixtures of iron and steel are attracted to a magnet.

Write each bold-faced word from above next to its meaning.

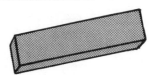

1. drawn to; pulled _____

2. cannot be seen _____

3. things that can be seen or touched _____

4. power to attract iron and steel _____

5. consisting of _____

Predict which of the following you think would be attracted by a magnet. Circle them. Check your predictions with a magnet.

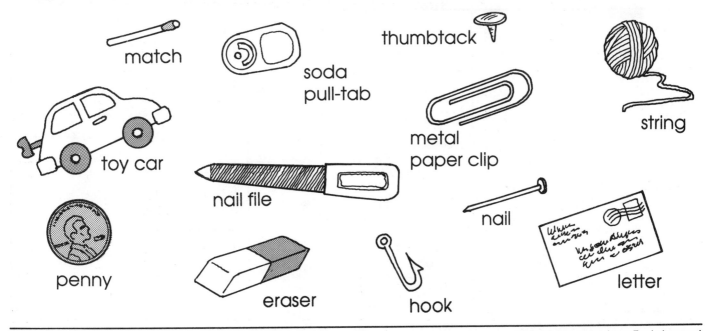

match

soda pull-tab

thumbtack

string

toy car

metal paper clip

nail file

nail

penny

eraser

hook

letter

Answer Key

Vocabulary Enrichment
Grade 2

Fine Feathered Friends

Name _____

Use the words from the Word Box to build a puzzle.
Hint: Build off **woodpecker** first.

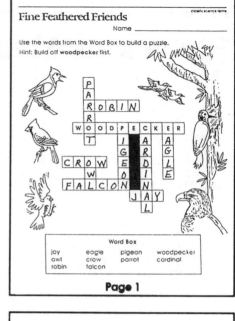

Word Box

jay	eagle	pigeon	woodpecker
owl	crow	parrot	cardinal
robin	falcon		

Page 1

Picture This

Name _____

Color the picture the bold-faced word tells about.

I will **coast** to the bottom of the hill.

The teacher said to **pass** the room quietly.

Barb lost the dollar **bill** she needed for lunch.

The glass was **shattered**.

Don is my **hero**.

Can you **field** a ball as good as Carlos?

Page 2

Mitten Match

Name _____

If the words on the pairs of mittens mean nearly the same thing, color the mittens. If they do not, put an X on the mittens.

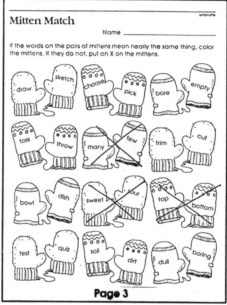

draw — sketch
choose — pick
bare — empty
toss — throw
many — few
trim — cut
bowl — dish
sweet — sour
top — bottom
test — quiz
soil — dirt
dull — boring

Page 3

Do You Know the Code?

Name _____

Use the code to write an antonym for each word.

t	r	s
c	h	a
n	e	i

Example: thick → ⌐ ☐ ⌐ ⌐ = thin

1. there → here
2. poor → rich
3. messy → neat
4. work → rest
5. unpleasant → nice
6. basement → attic
7. throw → catch

Page 4

Palindromes—Wow!

Name _____

A palindrome is a word that reads the same forward and backward. Use the code to write a palindrome for each word or phrase.
Example: short for sister = $\underline{S}_9 \underline{I}_4 \underline{S}_9$

Code	1	2	3	4	5	6	7	8	9	10	11
	a	d	e	i	l	m	n	o	p	s	t	u

1. mother = $\underline{m}_5 \underline{o}_7 \underline{m}_5$
2. father = $\underline{d}_2 \underline{a}_1 \underline{d}_2$
3. energy = $\underline{p}_8 \underline{e}_3 \underline{p}_8$
4. burst = $\underline{p}_8 \underline{o}_7 \underline{p}_8$
5. young dog = $\underline{p}_8 \underline{u}_{11} \underline{p}_8$
6. past tense of do = $\underline{d}_2 \underline{i}_4 \underline{d}_2$
7. midday = $\underline{n}_6 \underline{o}_7 \underline{o}_7 \underline{n}_6$
8. horn blast = $\underline{t}_{10} \underline{o}_7 \underline{o}_7 \underline{t}_{10}$

Page 5

At the Beach

Name _____

If the two words on a shell make a compound word, write them together on a line. Put an X on the shell if they do not make a compound word.

clam bake — clambake
sea shore — seashore
star fish — starfish
sea shell — seashell
sun burn — sunburn
swim suit — swimsuit
surf board — surfboard

Write a compound word from the list that is a synonym for beach.
seashore

Page 6

In a Nutshell

Name _____

Use the words from the Word Bank to build a puzzle.
Hint: Build off **chestnut** first.

Word Bank

acorn	pecan	almond	cashew
peanut	walnut	filbert	chestnut

Unscramble the letters to find another name for a filbert. Write it on the line.
hazelnut

Page 7

See You Later, Alligator

Name _____

If the pair of words on the alligator rhyme, color the alligator. If the words do not rhyme, put an X on the alligator.

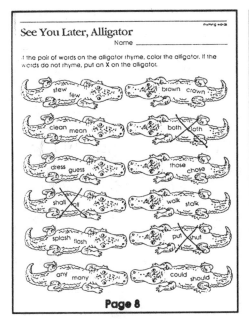

stew few — brown crown

clean mean — both ✗ loth

dress guess — those chose

shall ✗ all — walk stalk

splash flash — put ✗ shut

any many — could should

Page 8

A Day with Clay

Name _____

Choose the word that means nearly the same as the underlined word to complete each sentence. Write it in the blank.

I hope we <u>start</u> our art project today.

I want to __begin__ work now.
(begin, stop)

If I <u>finish</u> my clay bowl quickly, I'll have

time to __complete__ a vase, too.
(compare, complete)

I'll <u>send</u> the bowl to Grandma

and __mail__ the vase to Aunt Sue.
(mail, take)

Grandma could <u>place</u> the bowl on her

table or __set__ it on a shelf.
(sit, set)

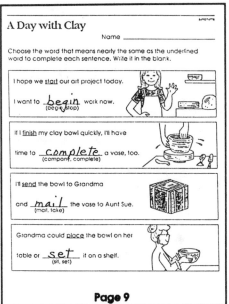

Page 9

Which Will You Pick?

Name _____

Rewrite each sentence, replacing the bold-faced word with another word that has the same meaning.

Word	Meanings	
peep	1. sound	2. look
pick	1. choose	2. gather
soft	1. low	2. not hard

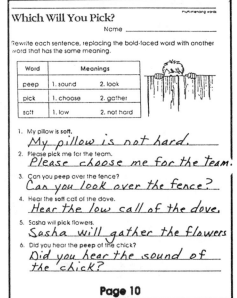

1. My pillow is **soft**.
   My pillow is not hard.
2. Please **pick** me for the team.
   Please choose me for the team.
3. Can you **peep** over the fence?
   Can you look over the fence?
4. Hear the **soft** call of the dove.
   Hear the low call of the dove.
5. Sasha will **pick** flowers.
   Sasha will gather the flowers
6. Did you hear the **peep** of the chick?
   Did you hear the sound of the chick?

Page 10

Unsolved Mystery

Name _____

If the pair of words on the magnifying glass are antonyms, write the letter from the handle above the matching numeral in the coded message. Put an X on the word pairs that are not antonyms.

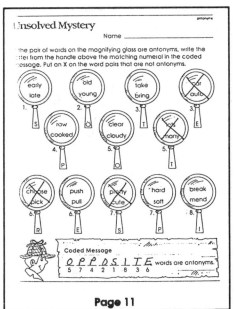

1. early late — S
2. old young — O
3. take bring — T
4. ✗ car auto — E
4. raw cooked — P
5. clear cloudy — O
6. ✗ look many — T
6. ✗ choose pick — R
6. push pull — E
7. ✗ pretty cute — S
7. hard soft — P
8. break mend — I

Coded Message
O P P O S I T E words are antonyms.
5 7 4 2 1 8 3 6

Page 11

Analyze These Analogies

Name _____

Write the correct word from the Word Box to complete each analogy.

Word Box				
eat	oink	brook	scales	color
sail	after	swamp	person	lemon

1. Gas is to car as food is to __person__
2. Milk is to drink as bread is to __eat__
3. Bee is to hive as alligator is to __swamp__
4. Hard is to soft as before is to __after__
5. Bear is to fur as fish is to __scales__
6. Cow is to moo as pig is to __oink__
7. Kite is to fly as boat is to __sail__
8. Road is to street as creek is to __brook__
9. Green is to lime as yellow is to __lemon__
10. Pencil is to write as crayon is to __color__

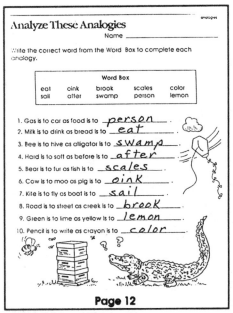

Page 12

Home Sweet Home

Name _____

Write the name of each animal's home below its picture. Then complete each sentence with the correct word.

Word Box					
hive	hutch	kennel	nest	stable	sty

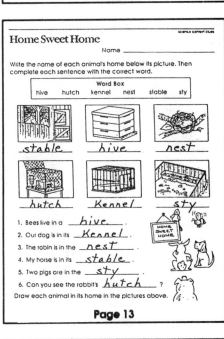

stable   hive   nest

hutch   kennel   sty

1. Bees live in a __hive__.
2. Our dog is in its __kennel__.
3. The robin is in the __nest__.
4. My horse is in its __stable__.
5. Two pigs are in the __sty__.
6. Can you see the rabbit's __hutch__?

Draw each animal in its home in the pictures above.

Page 13

How Do You Feel About This?

Name _____

In each oval, write a word from the Word Box that tells about the main idea.

Word Box			
sad	upset	grumpy	unhappy
glad	happy	loving	worried
caring	angry	joyful	cheerful

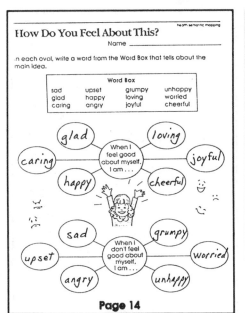

glad — loving
caring — When I feel good about myself. I am . . . — joyful
happy — cheerful

sad — grumpy
upset — When I don't feel good about myself, I am . . . — worried
angry — unhappy

Page 14

Try Hard on This

Name _____

Write the number of the correct definition for the bold-faced word in each sentence.

bite (bit) 1. cut with teeth 2. a piece bitten off 3. a sore from a bite

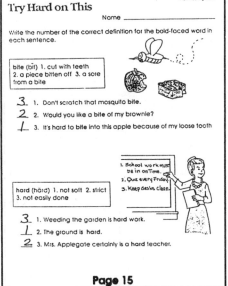

__3__ 1. Don't scratch that mosquito **bite**.
__2__ 2. Would you like a **bite** of my brownie?
__1__ 3. It's hard to **bite** into this apple because of my loose tooth

hard (härd) 1. not soft 2. strict 3. not easily done

__3__ 1. Weeding the garden is **hard** work.
__1__ 2. The ground is **hard**.
__2__ 3. Mrs. Applegate certainly is a **hard** teacher.

Page 15

You Don't Say!

Name _____

Rewrite the sentences using announced, answered, asked, begged or yelled instead of said.

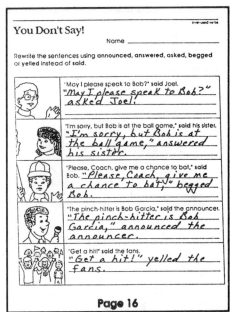

"May I please speak to Bob?" said Joel.
"May I please speak to Bob?" asked Joel.

"I'm sorry, but Bob is at the ball game," said his sister.
"I'm sorry, but Bob is at the ball game," answered his sister.

"Please, Coach, give me a chance to bat," said Bob.
"Please, Coach, give me a chance to bat," begged Bob.

"The pinch-hitter is Bob Garcia," said the announcer.
"The pinch-hitter is Bob Garcia," announced the announcer.

"Get a hit!" said the fans.
"Get a hit!" yelled the fans.

Page 16

Yummy for the Tummy
Name _____

Write the words from the Word Bx under the correct category name.
Then circle the words in the wordsearch. Look ↑ ↓ → ← ↘ ↙.

Word Box

apple	carrot	orange	peas
banana	cherry	peach	potato
beans	corn	pear	squash

Fruits		Vegetables	
apple	*orange*	*beans*	*peas*
banana	*peach*	*carrot*	*potato*
cherry	*pear*	*corn*	*squash*

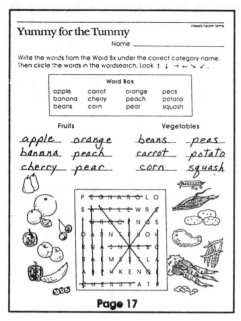

Page 17

Eating Out
Name _____

Circle the correct word and write it in the blank.

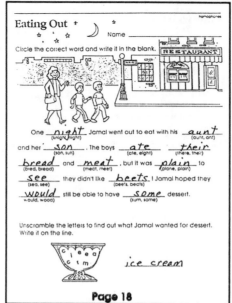

One __*night*__ Jamal went out to eat with his __*aunt*__
(knight, night)   (aunt, ant)
and her __*son*__. The boys __*ate*__ __*their*__
(son, sun)   (ate, eight)   (there, their)
__*bread*__ and __*meat*__, but it was __*plain*__ to
(bred, bread)   (meat, meet)   (plane, plain)
__*see*__ they didn't like __*beets*__ Jamal hoped they
(sea, see)   (bee's, beats)
__*would*__ still be able to have __*some*__ dessert.
(would, wood)   (sum, some)

Unscramble the letters to find out what Jamal wanted for dessert.
Write it on the line.

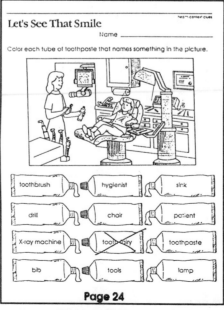

ice cream

Page 18

Synonym Switch
Name _____

Write a synonym for the word in the Column 1. Then change one
letter in that word to make a synonym for the word in **Column 2**.

Example: father mean
          d a d   b a d

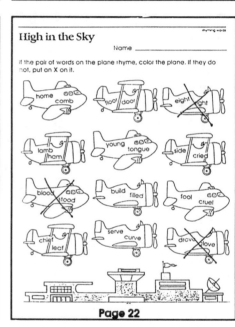

	Column 1	Column 2
	cool	grasp
1.	c o l d	h o l d
	carnival	den
2.	f l a i r	l a i r
	remain	swing
3.	s t a y	s w a y
	tale	shop
4.	s t o r y	s t o r e
	look	extra
5.	s t a r e	s p a r e
	powerful	cord
6.	s t r o n g	s t r i n g

Page 19

Word Problems
Name _____

Use words from the Word Box to complete these word equations. Add
two words that go with the first two words. Then write the category
name as the sum.

Word Box

behind	locations	postcard	aunt
sweater	messages	relatives	uncle
clothes	middle	slacks	card

Example: north + __east__
         south + __west__ = directions

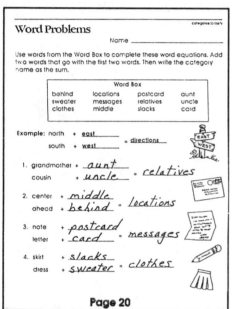

1. grandmother + __*aunt*__
   cousin + __*uncle*__ = __*relatives*__

2. center + __*middle*__
   ahead + __*behind*__ = __*locations*__

3. note + __*postcard*__
   letter + __*card*__ = __*messages*__

4. skirt + __*slacks*__
   dress + __*sweater*__ = __*clothes*__

Page 20

What Does It Mean?
Name _____

Read the meanings given for each word. Write the number of the
correct meaning of each bold-faced word in the circle.

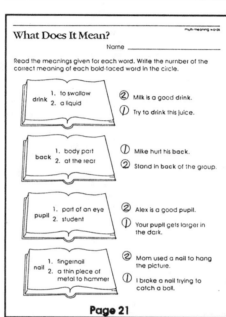

drink   1. to swallow   2. a liquid
② Milk is a good drink.
① Try to drink this juice.

back   1. body part   2. at the rear
① Mike hurt his back.
② Stand in back of the group.

pupil   1. part of an eye   2. student
② Alex is a good pupil.
① Your pupil gets larger in the dark.

nail   1. fingernail   2. a thin piece of metal to hammer
② Mom used a nail to hang the picture.
① I broke a nail trying to catch a ball.

Page 21

High in the Sky
Name _____

If the pair of words on the plane rhyme, color the plane. If they do
not, put an X on it.

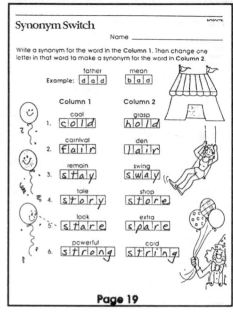

home / comb
floor / door (X) eight / light (X)
lamb / ham   young / tongue   side / cried
blood / stood (X)   build / filled   fool / cruel
chief / leaf   serve / curve   drove / love (X)

Page 22

Home Sweet Home
Name _____

Write the antonym from the Word Box for each word below. Then
circle the words from the Word Box in the wordsearch. Words may
go ↑ ↓ → ↘.

Word Box

| above | find | light | lower | weak |
| fancy | huge | love | shut | wrong |

1. dark __*light*__   6. below __*above*__
2. right __*wrong*__   7. strong __*weak*__
3. tiny __*huge*__   8. plain __*fancy*__
4. raise __*lower*__   9. lose __*find*__
5. hate __*love*__   10. open __*shut*__

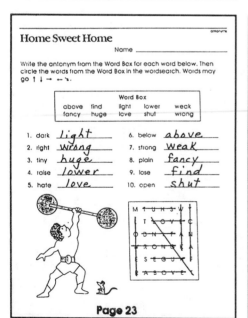

Page 23

Let's See That Smile
Name _____

Color each tube of toothpaste that names something in the picture.

toothbrush	hygienist	sink
drill	chair	patient
X-ray machine	tooth fairy	toothpaste
bib	tools	lamp

Page 24

Here's the Scoop!
Name _____

On each blank, write a word from the Word Box that comes between
the other two words in alphabetical order.

after / *before* / comb
fair / *frog* / gather
robin / *salad* / science

cane / *center* / chance
sink / *slide* / song

ticket / *touch* / travel
gentle / *gift* / grand
greet / *grind* / ground

| Word Box | center | before | frog | gift |
| | salad | touch | grind | slide |

Page 25

IF5022 Vocabulary Enrichment

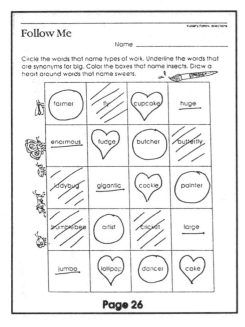

Follow Me

Name _____

Circle the words that name types of work. Underline the words that are synonyms for big. Color the boxes that name insects. Draw a heart around words that name sweets.

farmer	fly	cupcake	huge
enormous	fudge	butcher	butterfly
ladybug	gigantic	cockle	painter
bumblebee	artist	cricket	large
jumbo	lollipop	dancer	cake

Page 26

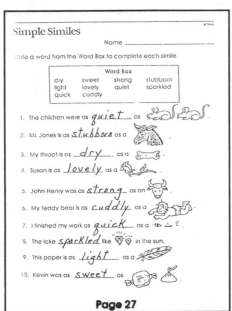

Simple Similes

Name _____

Write a word from the Word Box to complete each simile.

Word Box			
dry	sweet	strong	stubborn
light	lovely	quiet	sparkled
quick	cuddly		

1. The children were as _quiet_ as
2. Mr. Jones is as _stubborn_ as a
3. My throat is as _dry_ as a
4. Susan is as _lovely_ as a
5. John Henry was as _strong_ as an
6. My teddy bear is as _cuddly_ as a
7. I finished my work as _quick_ as a
8. The lake _sparkled_ like in the sun.
9. This paper is as _light_ as a
10. Kevin was as _sweet_ as

Page 27

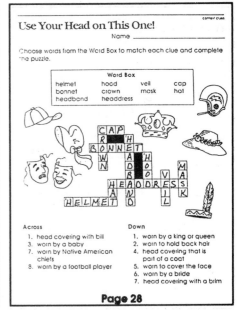

Use Your Head on This One!

Name _____

Choose words from the Word Box to match each clue and complete the puzzle.

Word Box			
helmet	hood	veil	cap
bonnet	crown	mask	hat
headband	headdress		

Across
1. head covering with bill
3. worn by a baby
7. worn by Native American chiefs
8. worn by a football player

Down
1. worn by a king or queen
2. worn to hold back hair
4. head covering that is part of a coat
5. worn to cover the face
6. worn by a bride
7. head covering with a brim

Page 28

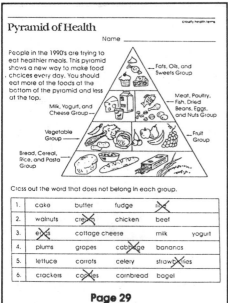

Pyramid of Health

Name _____

People in the 1990's are trying to eat healthier meals. This pyramid shows a new way to make food choices every day. You should eat more of the foods at the bottom of the pyramid and less at the top.

Fats, Oils, and Sweets Group

Milk, Yogurt, and Cheese Group

Meat, Poultry, Fish, Dried Beans, Eggs, and Nuts Group

Vegetable Group

Fruit Group

Bread, Cereal, Rice, and Pasta Group

Cross out the word that does not belong in each group.

1.	cake	butter	fudge	pie
2.	walnuts	cream	chicken	beef
3.	eggs	cottage cheese	milk	yogurt
4.	plums	grapes	cabbage	bananas
5.	lettuce	carrots	celery	strawberries
6.	crackers	cookies	cornbread	bagel

Page 29

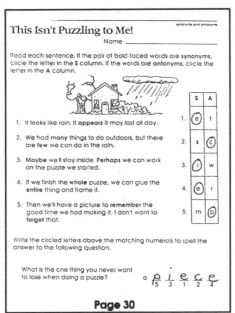

This Isn't Puzzling to Me!

Name _____

Read each sentence. If the pair of bold-faced words are synonyms, circle the letter in the S column. If the words are antonyms, circle the letter in the A column.

1. It looks like rain. It **appears** it may last all day.
2. We had **many** things to do outdoors, but there are **few** we can do in the rain.
3. **Maybe** we'll stay inside. **Perhaps** we can work on the puzzle we started.
4. If we finish the **whole** puzzle, we can glue the **entire** thing and frame it.
5. Then we'll have a picture to **remember** the good time we had making it. I don't want to **forget** that.

	S	A
1.	e	t
2.	s	c
3.	i	w
4.	e	r
5.	m	p

Write the circled letters above the matching numerals to spell the answer to the following question.

What is the one thing you never want to lose when doing a puzzle? a _p_ _i_ _e_ _c_ _e_
          5 3 1 2 4

Page 30

Piece Is to Puzzle

Name _____

Write a word in each puzzle to complete each analogy.

1. In is to out as stop is to . . .
2. She is to her as he is to . . .
3. House is to build as well is to . . .
4. Dog is to bark as lion is to . . .
5. Ceiling is to room as lid is to . . .
6. Much is to little as early is to . . .

Page 31

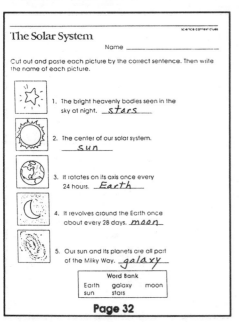

The Solar System

Name _____

Cut out and paste each picture by the correct sentence. Then write the name of each picture.

1. The bright heavenly bodies seen in the sky at night. _stars_
2. The center of our solar system. _sun_
3. It rotates on its axis once every 24 hours. _Earth_
4. It revolves around the Earth once about every 28 days. _moon_
5. Our sun and its planets are all part of the Milky Way. _galaxy_

Word Bank		
Earth	galaxy	moon
sun	stars	

Page 32

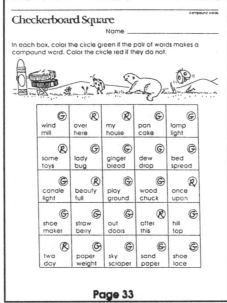

Checkerboard Square

Name _____

In each box, color the circle green if the pair of words makes a compound word. Color the circle red if they do not.

wind mill	over here	my house	pan cake	lamp light
some toys	lady bug	ginger bread	dew drop	bed spread
candle light	beauty full	play ground	wood chuck	once upon
shoe maker	straw berry	out doors	after this	hill top
two day	paper weight	sky scraper	sand paper	shoe lace

Page 33

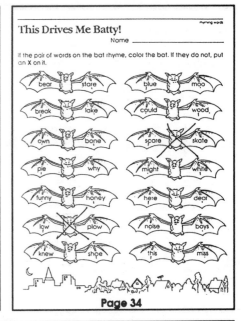

This Drives Me Batty!

Name _____

If the pair of words on the bat rhyme, color the bat. If they do not, put an X on it.

bear	stare	blue	moo
break	lake	could	wood
own	bone	scare	skate
pie	why	might	white
funny	honey	here	deal
low	plow	noise	boys
knew	shoe	this	miss

Page 34

IF5022 Vocabulary Enrichment

Once Upon a Time
Name _____

Circle the correct word and write it in the blank.

Mr. Hill, the librarian, read __our__ (hour, out) class a story about a

__prince__ (prince, prints) and a __fairy__ (ferry, fairy) godmother. We __knew__ (knew, new) a

story about a godmother, but __we'd__ (weed, we'd) never __heard__ (herd, heard) this

__one__ (won, one) before. It was such a __great__ (great, grate) __tale__ (tale, tail) that

we weren't __bored__ (bored, board). We asked Mr. Hill to let us __hear__ (hear, here)

it again. He said that we had __been__ (bin, been) good listeners, but he

did __not__ (not, knot) have time to read it again.

Page 35

Join the Community
Name _____

Use words from the Word Box to complete each sentence. Then write those words in the puzzle.

Word Box
council   laws   taxes
problems   rules   mayor
leaders   city   vote
services

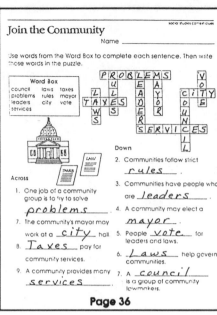

Across
1. One job of a community group is to try to solve __problems__
7. The community's mayor may work at a __city__ hall.
8. __Taxes__ pay for community services.
9. A community provides many __services__

Down
2. Communities follow strict __rules__
3. Communities have people who are __leaders__
4. A community may elect a __mayor__.
5. People __vote__ for leaders and laws.
6. __Laws__ help govern communities.
7. A __council__ is a group of community lawmakers.

Page 36

Unlock These Words
Name _____

Write the pronunciation for each word in bold-faced type.

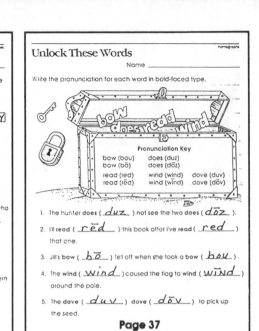

Pronunciation Key
bow (bou)   does (duz)
bow (bō)   does (dōz)
read (red)   wind (wind)   dove (duv)
read (rēd)   wind (wīnd)   dove (dōv)

1. The hunter does (__duz__) not see the two does (__dōz__).
2. I'll read (__rēd__) this book after I've read (__red__) that one.
3. Jill's bow (__bō__) fell off when she took a bow (__bou__).
4. The wind (__wind__) caused the flag to wind (__wīnd__) around the pole.
5. The dove (__duv__) dove (__dōv__) to pick up the seed.

Page 37

You'll Shine on This!
Name _____

Write a word from the design to complete each analogy. Write it. Then color that word's space yellow.

1. Puppy is to dog as kitten is to __cat__
2. Boot is to foot as glove is to __hand__
3. Sun is to hot as snow is to __cold__
4. Boy is to girl as brother is to __sister__
5. Den is to bear as hive is to __bee__
6. Breakfast is to morning as dinner is to __evening__
7. Bird is to sky as fish is to __water__
8. Pretty is to lovely as wise is to __smart__
9. Fast is to slow as high is to __low__
10. Plane is to pilot as car is to __driver__

Color the remaining spaces blue.

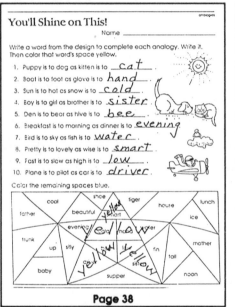

Page 38

Batter Up!
Name _____

Read the meanings given for each word. On the line, write the correct meaning of the word as it is used in each sentence.

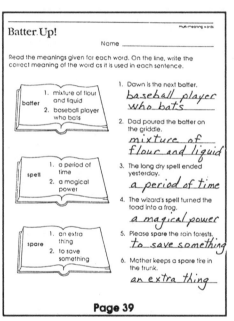

batter
1. mixture of flour and liquid
2. baseball player who bats

spell
1. a period of time
2. a magical power

spare
1. an extra thing
2. to save something

1. Down is the next batter.
__baseball player who bats__

2. Dad poured the batter on the griddle.
__mixture of flour and liquid__

3. The long dry spell ended yesterday.
__a period of time__

4. The wizard's spell turned the toad into a frog.
__a magical power__

5. Please spare the rain forests.
__to save something__

6. Mother keeps a spare tire in the trunk.
__an extra thing__

Page 39

This Is Pretty Nice!
Name _____

Find a new word from the Word Box to use instead of the bold-faced word in each sentence. Write the new words in the puzzle.

Word Box
cute   lovely   enjoyable   attractive
fine   proper   adorable   beautiful
kind   pleasing

Across
3. Marla is a pretty girl.
6. That kitten is pretty.
7. That is not a nice way to behave!
8. You are so nice to me.
9. The new curtains are pretty.
10. That rose is pretty.

Down
1. What a pretty baby!
2. That painting is nice to look at.
4. This is a nice picnic.
5. Eric is a nice person.

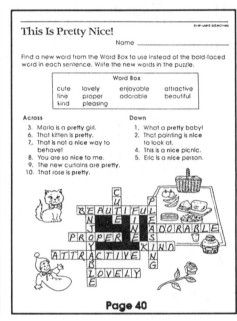

Page 40

As Tough As Nails
Name _____

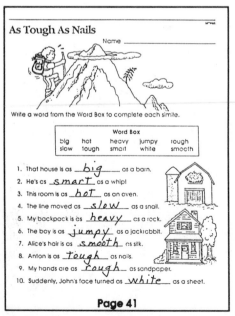

Write a word from the Word Box to complete each simile.

Word Box
big   hot   heavy   jumpy   rough
slow   tough   smart   white   smooth

1. That house is as __big__ as a barn.
2. He's as __smart__ as a whip!
3. This room is as __hot__ as an oven.
4. The line moved as __slow__ as a snail.
5. My backpack is as __heavy__ as a rock.
6. The boy is as __jumpy__ as a jackrabbit.
7. Alice's hair is as __smooth__ as silk.
8. Anton is as __tough__ as nails.
9. My hands are as __rough__ as sandpaper.
10. Suddenly, John's face turned as __white__ as a sheet.

Page 41

Super Synonyms
Name _____

Use words from the Word Box to write synonyms for each pair of words. Then write each numbered letter in the box with the same number. You'll spell a synonym for the word above the boxes.

silly

Word Box
assist   right   similar   trip
rescue   weird   fearless   silly

strange __weird__
1 2 3 4 5

journey __trip__
6 4 3 7

sleepy __tired__
6 3 4 2 5

brave __fearless__
1 2 3 4 5 2 6 6

steps __stairs__
6 8 3 7 4 6

help __assist__
3 6 6 7 6 8

foolish __silly__
1 2 3 4

ring __circle__
7 2 5 7 3 6

save __rescue__
5 6 1 7 8 6

correct __right__
1 2 4 5

wise __smart__
6 7 9 1 5

alike __similar__
6 2 7 2 8 9 1

Page 42

Marvelous Magnets
Name _____

Some things are pulled, or attracted, by a magnet. Other objects are not. Because magnetism is invisible, you cannot tell if an object is magnetic just by looking at it. Things containing mixtures of iron and steel are attracted to a magnet.

Write each bold-faced word from above next to its meaning.

1. drawn to; pulled __attracted__
2. cannot be seen __invisible__
3. things that can be seen or touched __objects__
4. power to attract iron and steel __magnetism__
5. consisting of __containing__

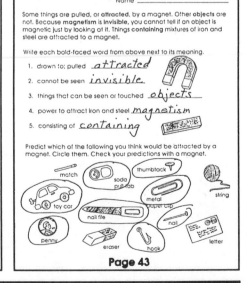

Predict which of the following you think would be attracted by a magnet. Circle them. Check your predictions with a magnet.

Page 43
